I Am

I Am

Stories from the Gospel of John

Written by
Laura Cerbus
Illustrated by
Lee Dixon

10 Publishing
a division of 10ofthose.com

First published in Great Britain in 2025

British Library Cataloguing in Publication Data
A record for this book is available from the British Library

ISBN: 978-1-91496-682-8

Designed and typeset by Pete Barnsley (CreativeHoot.com)
Illustrations by Lee Dixon

Printed in Denmark

10Publishing, a division of 10ofthose.com
Unit C, Tomlinson Road, Leyland, PR25 2DY, England

info@10ofthose.com
www.10ofthose.com

1 3 5 7 10 8 6 4 2

CONTENTS

PREFACE

The stories of Jesus are some of the most famous stories in the Bible. Each gospel writer crafted their narratives from their perspective, drawing attention to different aspects of Jesus' identity and mission. The apostle John wrote his own account of Jesus' life and ministry. In these pages, you will find retellings of a series of stories that John recorded—stories all connected by Jesus' declaration, "I AM." In these stories, Jesus speaks about his identity as the Messiah for whom God's people had been waiting.

The Old Testament is full of images and promises that pointed God's people ahead in time, to the arrival of Jesus. They spoke of who Jesus would be, and what he would do. When Jesus did come, he connected his identity and his actions with those Old Testament images and promises.

These retellings of John's stories imagine what he might have thought and felt as he followed Jesus. They imagine what it would have been like for him to sit under Jesus' teaching, to witness Jesus' miracles—and they invite you to imagine, as well. Who might you be, in these stories? And more importantly, how will you respond to Jesus?

How to use this book

This book is designed for children and those who want to share Jesus' stories with them. Children can navigate the stories independently, or alongside someone older. The stories can be read through and enjoyed as a whole, or they can be used devotionally, worked through one at a time. After each story, you will find short sections titled "Growing Deeper". These sections provide some further explanation of the ideas in Jesus' stories and make connections to readers today. Finally, each story closes with a short prayer.

My prayer for each of you is that in these stories, you will be drawn to Jesus—the bread of life; the light of the world; the great I AM; the gate; the shepherd; the resurrection and the life; the way, truth, and life; the vine. May you know the life that comes through him.

JOHN MEETS JESUS

God's people were waiting. God had spoken to the Israelites through his prophets, and he had brought them into the promised land. But now, hundreds of years had passed since God had spoken to them through a prophet. Where was God's word—his promises, his instruction, his presence? Why was God far off? Would he be silent forever?

Hundreds of years had passed since the Israelites had ruled their own land in peace and safety. Wave after wave of foreign nations had invaded them, sometimes carrying them off to faraway lands, and now the empire of Rome ruled over their land. The Romans put their own governors in place to rule the people. The Israelites knew that the Roman ruler was not the good king that God had promised. They were still allowed to worship God, but they needed to obey Rome's laws and pay Rome's taxes.

A man named John was waiting, too. A Jewish man from Galilee, he knew the promises that God had given his people hundreds of years ago. Through the prophets, God had promised to restore them, to bring them back to himself and his ways, after they had broken his covenant with them. He had promised to defeat his and their enemies. In these promises, God gave his people pictures and signs that pointed to one who was to come. This one, the Messiah, would fulfill the promises God had made to them. But when, John wondered, would these promises come to pass?

One day, news of a prophet near Jerusalem reached John. John thought, *Did this new prophet have a word from God after so many years?* The rumors were that the prophet lived in the wilderness outside of Jerusalem, preaching and baptizing people in the Jordan River. They said that he survived on a diet of locusts and honey. Curious, John left his home in Galilee. He traveled south, towards Jerusalem, following the Jordan.

John traveled for almost a week on foot, his sandaled feet crunching against the rocky path. As he walked, he thought about his people, who had been waiting for so long. Without a word from God, the present looked dark and without hope.

Some of John's people had tried to take things into their own hands, resisting the Romans who ruled over them. These were the Zealots, a group eager to rebel against the Romans and take their land back by force.

Some of them were determined to hold onto their identity as God's people. They tried to do this by setting up rules and regulations to keep God's people pure and separate from the Romans and others around them who were not Jewish. These men, the Pharisees, were the religious leaders of God's people.

Some of them, John thought, *had forgotten what they were waiting for.*

When John found the prophet, he was not alone. Crowds of people had followed the prophet into the wilderness—people who were curious, perhaps, like John. He was called the Baptizer, because he was washing people in the Jordan as a sign of their repentance and desire to get ready for the Messiah.

John looked at the river—muddy and still, it did not look like the best place to wash oneself. But John remembered the story of the army captain, Naaman, who at first scoffed at cleansing in such an unpromising river. When Naaman finally did, he was cured of his leprosy.

Today, the prophet stood next to the river, his voice raised as he spoke to the crowd gathered around him. He was calling for repentance, for people to turn away from their sins.

His camel-hair coat tied around the waist with a leather belt contrasted strongly with the softer woven clothing of those in the crowd. Between his clothing and his diet, the prophet was clearly no ordinary person—*but,* John thought, *neither were the prophets from long ago.*

At a lull in the prophet's preaching, a group of men pushed through to confront him. A whisper went through the crowd: these men were from Jerusalem, sent by the Pharisees.

"Who are you?" the men asked.

In response, the prophet repeated the words of another prophet, a man called Isaiah. "I am a voice shouting in the wilderness," he said. "Clear the way for the Lord's coming!"

The prophet was preparing the way for someone—someone important.

John decided to stay, his curiosity still not satisfied. He wanted to hear more about the one the prophet was preparing for. He met others who followed the prophet, eager for repentance and for the Messiah that he promised would come.

One day, a man came to the Jordan River. The man was a carpenter from Nazareth, a man called Jesus. When the prophet saw him, he pointed to Jesus and cried, "Look! There is the **LAMB OF GOD!**"

What an astonishing claim, John thought. *What could it mean? Who was this man? Could he be the answer to the longings of God's people? Could he be the one they were waiting for?*

John had to find out.

"Rabbi, where are you staying?" he and his friend Andrew asked Jesus.

"**COME AND SEE**," Jesus replied.

John and Andrew followed Jesus to where he was staying. They stayed with him that day—and the

next. Others joined them. Together, they became Jesus' disciples.

When John turned his feet to follow Jesus, his whole life changed. John would see one boy's lunch multiplied to feed thousands; he would smell a man who had been dead for four days, only to be raised to life; he would hear words powerful enough to cause many to follow Jesus and others to plot to kill him.

Many years later, John wrote about what he saw and heard at Jesus' side. God had not forgotten his people, and in Jesus, his true Word, he fulfilled all the promises he had made long ago. These promises are not only for the Israelites—they are for all of God's people, for you and me today.

Come and see.

PRAYER

Lord, you who have not forgotten your people. Teach us to wait patiently for you. Encourage our hearts with the stories of how you have kept your promises through Jesus.

Amen.

1

I AM THE BREAD OF LIFE

"Blasphemer!" the Pharisees called Jesus. They knew what he was claiming by calling God his Father. John could see the way they looked at the people who surrounded him. John knew they thought this teacher had fooled everyone—except for them.

Yet Jesus continued to press the Pharisees, trying to get them to see that they couldn't love the Father, and they couldn't believe Moses, if they didn't love and believe him.

John was exhausted. He could see that Jesus was, too. All day, Jesus had been busy healing the sick, and he had talked and talked with the Pharisees. Although the Pharisees kept coming back to Jesus, they weren't Jesus' followers. Their stern looks, downturned mouths, and stiff postures spoke loud and clear of their hostility to Jesus.

Finally, Jesus managed to slip away from the religious leaders and the crowds. With a few of the disciples trailing behind him, holding the crowds back, Jesus was able to find his way out of the town and into the countryside. Glancing behind him every so often to make sure they

weren't being followed, John walked closely behind Jesus as he headed for the other side of the Sea of Galilee. He hoped that Jesus would choose a quiet spot, hidden away from any persistent people.

Soon, Jesus veered off the path that wrapped around the sea and started climbing a hill that rose up from near the shoreline. John stifled a groan as he looked at the steep incline. He was not sure his legs could carry him any further.

With relief, he saw Jesus stop and sit down. As John sat down after him, his whole body sank into the grass. The others sighed, too, as they stretched out their weary legs and feet. No one spoke and, as John felt his breathing slow, he allowed his eyes to close. The sound of waves slapping at the shore faded as he drifted off.

A sharp cry broke through his sleepiness and John's eyes flew open. One of the disciples was pointing back the way they had come. John sat up to follow his line of sight. A groan broke free from his lips, too—

in the distance, a crowd of people were tracing the path they had taken along the lake. Soon, the crowd would reach them.

By now, the others had seen the crowd as well and, by their slumped shoulders and weary eyes, John knew they felt like he did. He briefly thought of suggesting that they hide, but he knew that Jesus would not take that suggestion. Surely, though, Jesus would send the crowd away.

He glanced over at Jesus. John saw no trace of annoyance or frustration on his face.

As the crowd came closer, Jesus turned to Phillip. "Where can we buy bread to feed all these people?" he asked.

John and the disciples looked at the crowd. They looked at each other. Was Jesus serious? They began to worry. "Even if we worked for months, we wouldn't have enough money to feed them!" Philip told Jesus.

Jesus wasn't worried.

By now, the crowd had gathered around Jesus. A few of the disciples began to work their way through the people, wanting to see if they had brought food with them. Were they hungry? John heard his own stomach growl and guessed that they would be.

In the crowd, Andrew found a young boy who was happy to share his lunch: five loaves of barley bread and two fish. He offered his simple lunch to Jesus.

The disciples looked at the bread and the fish, and they looked at the crowd. Thousands of people had gathered around them. Offering so little food to that many people would be like offering a crumb of bread to a flock of birds. No one would get enough.

Still, Jesus gave instructions. "Tell everyone to sit down," he said to his disciples. Again, the disciples looked at each other. They could not imagine what

Jesus was planning. This time, though, they said nothing. Splitting up, they walked through the crowd and instructed everyone to sit.

The people listened to the disciples and sat down on the grass that covered the hill. Then, Jesus took the boy's loaves, thanked his Father for them, and turned to the crowd with the loaves and fish.

To each person, Jesus gave as much as they wanted. Then, he reached for more—and more was always there. The food which the disciples had counted—five loaves, two fish—continued to multiply as Jesus moved through the crowd.

When Jesus came to John, offering him a piece of bread and fish, John hesitated at first. If he took what Jesus was offering, would there be enough for the others? A hungry crowd was not something John wanted to face. But Jesus offered again, and then John realized that no one around him was going hungry. Somehow, there was enough.

When he was finished, Jesus told the disciples to gather up the leftovers.

Leftovers? John thought. Still, he obeyed. Soon, he needed a basket: he couldn't hold all of the leftovers in his hands. He wasn't the only one. When they met back with Jesus, the disciples had collected twelve baskets of food. They held the abundance of Jesus' miracle in their hands.

Such a miracle didn't go unnoticed. The excitement rippled through the crowd as the people shared their astonishment—so much food! And so much left over! The crowd knew that Jesus was the one they were waiting for.

But the next day, when Jesus spoke of himself as the one God had sent, the people resisted. Even with their stomachs full on Jesus' miracle, the people still demanded more proof.

"Show us a miraculous sign!" they said. "What can you do? After all, our ancestors ate manna while they journeyed through the wilderness! The Scriptures say, 'Moses gave them bread from heaven to eat.'"

At this request, John turned quickly towards Jesus. What would he say to this? He had just given them more than they could eat, and they still wanted more?

"Moses didn't give you bread from heaven," Jesus reminded them. "My Father did. And now he offers you the true bread from heaven. The true bread of God is the one who comes down from heaven and gives life to the world."

Then he told them, "I AM THE BREAD OF LIFE."

"Whoever comes to me," Jesus said, "will never be hungry again. Whoever believes in me will never be thirsty."

John thought about the baskets full of bread and fish that they had collected yesterday. He wondered about Jesus' promise. Would he continue to provide food for them, like God had provided for the Israelites in the desert so long ago? Was the bread and fish Jesus' way of giving them manna and quail?

But manna and quail, just like bread and fish, wouldn't stop him from being hungry again.

And Jesus' words confused him. He had said, "I AM the bread that came down from heaven."

Jesus' claim wasn't that he would provide bread, but that he *was* bread. John puzzled over this answer. Yes, he believed that Jesus had come from God, but how would Jesus *be* bread? More questions than answers swirled around in John's head—but Jesus continued to speak.

"I AM THE LIVING BREAD that came down from heaven," Jesus told the people. "Anyone who eats this bread will live forever; and this bread, which I will offer so the world may live, is my flesh."

John looked around him. Did anyone else think this sounded as crazy as he did? He kept his confusion to himself, but others didn't. Some argued among themselves, asking how Jesus could possibly give them his flesh to eat.

Jesus heard their arguments, but he pressed on. "I tell you the truth, unless you eat the flesh of the Son of Man and drink his blood, you cannot have eternal life within you."

As Jesus spoke, the crowd became restless. John saw his own confusion on their faces. Yet, they questioned something that John did not: they wondered about how Jesus could have come down from heaven, because they knew Jesus' mother and father. They knew Mary and Joseph, and so they scoffed at Jesus' claim that he came from heaven.

John did not yet understand what Jesus meant about eating his body and drinking his blood. For now, though, knowing that Jesus was from God, that Jesus was the one his people had been waiting for, was enough. His heart was being drawn to Jesus, and he would continue to follow him.

GROWING DEEPER

JOHN 6:1–59

When the people asked Jesus for manna, they remembered the bread that their ancestors ate in the wilderness. But manna wasn't the only kind of food that they needed. They—and we!—also needed spiritual food that gives eternal life and sustains our faith. When Jesus told the people, "I AM THE BREAD OF LIFE," he was saying, "I AM the food that you need for spiritual life."

In the desert, Satan tempted Jesus to satisfy his own hunger by turning a rock into bread. But Jesus didn't come to satisfy himself. He came to give himself up. He gave his own body to us to be our bread. He gave his body to us on the cross, giving up his life so that we could have life. When we come to Jesus, when we believe that he is who he says he is, we don't hold him at arm's length. What you eat becomes a part of you: your body digests it and is strengthened by it. When Jesus is our bread, we have eternal life—abundant, bellies-full life.

The people wanted to know what Jesus could do for them: they wanted to always have food to eat, and they wanted to see more miracles. Jesus told them that wasn't the most important thing. The most important thing is who Jesus is. Jesus could give them more food, but they would just get hungry again. They didn't need more loaves and fish—they needed him.

PRAYER

Lord, you are the bread of life. We come to you needy, hungry for you to sustain our life, to renew our faith in you. Help us to turn to you to satisfy all our needs.

Amen.

2

I AM THE LIGHT OF THE WORLD

As John wound his way through the streets of Jerusalem, he had to keep a close eye on Jesus in order not to lose him. The crowds pressed close on every side, their shouts filling their air.

The other disciples followed as well, moving closer and then farther away from John as they threaded their way through the crowds. The number of people surprised John; now, days after the Feast of Booths, most of the pilgrims who had traveled to Jerusalem to celebrate should be on their way home.

Jesus' path took them towards the temple. As they approached, John began to smell whiffs of the burnt offerings, especially the sweetness of the meat as it met the flames of the altar. The crowds' noise drowned out any other sound, but John imagined he could hear the bleating of goats and the lowing of bulls kept waiting for their turn.

John was so focused on the back of Jesus' head, he saw the willow branch only just in time to duck before it swatted him in the face. The branch

stuck out from the otherwise well-woven roof of the temporary booth built in the street. It had surprised John because, since the end of the feast, most of the booths had been taken down already. Just a few days before, the streets had been lined with hundreds of other booths built with tree branches of willow and olive, and decorated with grape vines and fruit.

Having successfully dodged the protruding branch, John relaxed as he saw the crowds thin out in front of him. The disciples now walked closer together, and John was able to ease his focus on Jesus. As he did, his mind wandered. The stray booth reminded him of the booths he had built over the years with his family. He remembered his father's instruction about their three-sided booth. It needed to be sturdy, able to survive a week-long celebration of feasting and revelry, and shady, providing good protection from the strengthening springtime sun, as well as allowing the night stars to shine through. He remembered his excitement as he and his siblings filled the booth with cushions for reclining around the table, making it ready for the guests they would entertain there. He remembered his mother's voice, narrating the story he and his siblings could recite themselves by the time they were grown.

We celebrate the Feast of Tabernacles each year in thanksgiving to God for his provision, John narrated as his mother's voice echoed in his memory. *At the end of the harvest, we give thanks for the crops God has blessed us with. But that's not all. Sukkot is also a feast of memory: we remember our ancestors and their wanderings in the wilderness. Forty years they wandered with Moses, and forty years God provided for them. While they wandered,*

they lived in tents, like this booth. No homes of mud or brick—nothing permanent. With this booth, we remember our dependence on God. We look for his deliverance, as God delivered our ancestors from Egypt.

John's thoughts came quickly back to the present as the temple came into view, and as Jesus stopped walking. John exhaled as his feet came to rest.

Soon, the people around them took notice: many of them recognized Jesus. He and the disciples had been in Jerusalem for over a week now. They had come up to Jerusalem, like the other pilgrims, to celebrate the feast. Jesus had already been to the temple to teach, and his words had provoked the Pharisees and the crowds. Now, news of his coming again to the temple traveled quickly. A crowd began to gather, curious as to what he might say this time. John and the disciples began to form a loose ring around Jesus, worried that the crowds might press in on him. As they did so, Jesus began to speak.

"I AM the light of the world. If you follow me, you won't have to walk in darkness, because you will have the light that leads to life."

Light. John's eyes instantly darted to the lampstands in the temple courtyard. They were extinguished now, because it was daytime, but the priests had lit them each night of the feast the week before. They towered over the courtyard, each with four branches and bowls for oil. John remembered the way the light had illuminated

the city. Like the booths, the light reminded John and the Jewish people of the memories passed down from their ancestors.

John remembered the stories: the story of the pillar of fire that God had provided for his people to light their way through the darkness of the wilderness. The stories of a temple once filled with God's glory, in the time before the exile. Surely Jesus knew these stories, too.

The image of light began to fill John's mind with even more stories. His thoughts went all the way back to the beginning, God's very first words of creation: "Let there be light!" Words which illuminated the world, creating the sun and through it the light and heat, which would coax tiny plants to push through the ground and unfurl their tender leaves.

Then he thought of King David's songs that they continued to sing, the songs that declared, "The Lord is my light and my salvation," and "The Lord, my God, lights up my darkness." So many songs about God being their light, showing them the way, and saving them.

And the prophet Isaiah spoke about light, too! Didn't Isaiah prophesy that, "The people who walk in darkness will see a great light. For those who live in a land of deep darkness, a light will shine"? It was definitely a dark time for God's people, with the Romans occupying their land and the glory of God's

presence gone from the temple. *Is now*, John wondered, *the time that Isaiah spoke of?*

GROWING DEEPER

JOHN 8:12–20

"I AM the light of the world," Jesus said. And it's true! He is the light of the *whole* world—not Israel alone, not only those twelve small tribes and their children's children's children. God had promised Abraham, "In you all the families of the earth shall be blessed." And through Isaiah, God promised that his people would be "a light to the nations."

What joy John must have felt when they recognized Jesus in all of these stories and songs and prophecies! What joy to realize that God's light had not gone out, but that it had come in glory and power to shine on the whole world and overcome the darkness in their world and in their hearts.

And in *our* world and in *our* hearts, too. Jesus, God's light, has conquered the darkness. Sometimes darkness still tries to creep in and extinguish the light, but it won't win. Wherever we see the darkness take hold, wherever we see lies and oppression and selfishness and greed, we can know that Jesus has broken their power, and we can be bold to say so. And when we look in our own hearts, and see the darkness of sin and selfishness, we can look to Jesus. It's only through him that we can see ourselves as we really are and be saved.

PRAYER

Lord, as the light of the world, shine in our hearts and in our world. Reveal our sin for what it is, and turn us towards you, as we trust in you to conquer the darkness. Amen.

3

BEFORE ABRAHAM WAS, I AM

Who is Jesus? Again and again, John heard the people that met Jesus ask this question. They had heard about him or listened to him teach or watched

him perform miracles, and all of it led to the question, "Who are you?" Sometimes it was said in wonder, in awe, in breathless hope at what the answer might be. And sometimes it was said in suspicion, in jealousy, or even hatred.

One day, Jesus spoke to the crowds around him about his relationship with his Father.

"I do nothing on my own," Jesus said, "but say only what the Father taught me. And the one who sent me is with me—he has not deserted me. For I always do what pleases him."

This time, the people responded positively to Jesus. John saw their eager faces and heard their excited chatter as they conferred with friends who had come with them, or with strangers also amazed at Jesus' claims. *Belief*! John thought. *They understand who Jesus is*.

These people were not ones to leave after listening briefly. Instead, they stayed, wanting to hear more from Jesus, wanting to become his disciples. So, Jesus continued to teach.

He told them, "You are truly my disciples if you remain faithful to my teachings. And you will know the truth, and the truth will set you free."

Some interrupted. "But we are descendants of Abraham," they said. "We have never been slaves to anyone. What do you mean, 'You will be set free'?"

Jesus replied, "I tell you the truth, everyone who sins is a slave of sin. A slave is not a permanent member of the family, but a son is part of the family forever. So, if the Son sets you free, you are truly free. I AM telling you what I saw when I was with my Father. But you are following the advice of your father."

"Our father is Abraham!" they declared.

"No," Jesus replied, "for if you were really the children of Abraham, you would follow his example. Instead, you are trying to kill me because I told you the truth, which I heard from God. Abraham

never did such a thing. No, you are imitating your real father."

Again, the people protested. John could see their faces begin to change—brows furrowed and mouths turned down. They were not happy with what Jesus had said, especially when he continued to insist that God was not their Father.

Jesus told them, "If God were your Father, you would love me, because I have come to you from God. I AM not here on my own, but he sent me. Why can't you understand what I AM saying? It's because you can't even hear me!"

John was surprised. Hadn't these people just expressed their belief in Jesus? Didn't they want to follow him? How could Jesus dismiss what they had said?

Jesus continued speaking. "For you are the children of your father the devil, and you love to do the evil

things he does. Anyone who belongs to God listens gladly to the words of God. But you don't listen because you don't belong to God."

These words shocked John—and the people, too. They hurled insults at Jesus: "You Samaritan devil! Didn't we say all along that you were possessed by a demon?"

Jesus did not flinch. "No," Jesus said, "I have no demon in me. For I honor my Father—and you dishonor me. I tell you the truth, anyone who obeys my teaching will never die!"

The people said, "Now we know you are possessed by a demon. Even Abraham and the prophets died, but you say, 'Anyone who obeys my teaching will never die!' Are you greater than our father Abraham? He died, and so did the prophets. Who do you think you are?"

Jesus claimed to come from God his Father, to be sent by him. He told the people that Abraham had been looking forward to the day when Jesus would come.

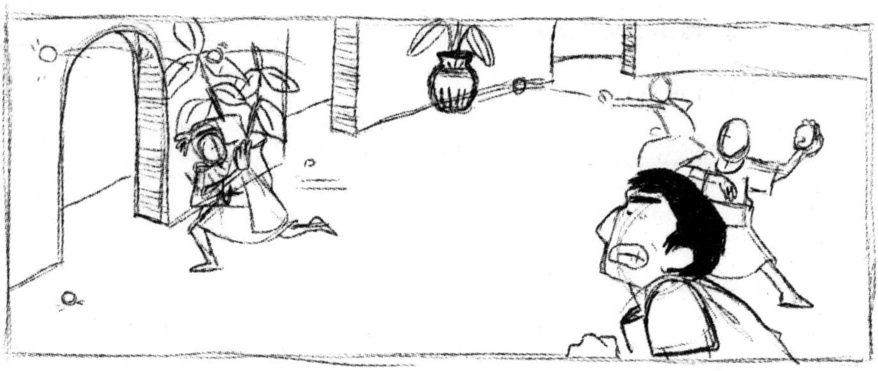

"I tell you the truth," said Jesus, "before Abraham was even born, I AM."

At these words, the people lost control. Fear struck John's heart as he realized how angry they were. With faces distorted in anger, they shouted out at Jesus. Some of them raised their fists, and others pointed stiff fingers accusingly at Jesus. And then, to John's horror, some of them reached down, searching the ground for stones. John instinctively raised one arm to protect his face, even as he realized that he was not their target.

The crowd surged forward, cutting John off from Jesus. The stones flew from their hands, some hitting the surrounding stone wall with a sharp crack, others landing on the ground with a dull thud.

None of them hit their mark. Jesus slipped away, escaping from the temple.

GROWING DEEPER

JOHN 8:48–59

What had happened? Why were the people so angry at Jesus' words?

You see, Jesus did not say to them, "Before Abraham was, I was." That would have been an amazing statement—Jesus claiming to be alive for thousands of years. But Jesus was claiming much more. In the words,, "I AM," Jesus took the people all the way back to the time of Moses, to the burning bush. There, in a bush caught on fire but not burning up, God revealed his character to Moses. Moses wanted to know who was speaking to him, who was telling him to go and bring the Israelites out of Egypt. So, God declared his name to Moses: "I AM WHO I AM."

I AM: God is without beginning or end. God without change.

Jesus is this God. I've been here all along, Jesus was telling them. In the stories of God's people, I was there.

Jesus, the eternal Word of God, is the one by whom all things were made. The one who was with God and was God in the beginning. Jesus is the promised one to whom all of the faithful believers in the Old Testament looked. He was the object of their faith, hope, and salvation. Jesus, the eternal Son of God, has been and is and will be with God in all of his glory and majesty and divinity. God of God, Light of Light, very God of very God. One with the Father, not less in any way.

PRAYER

Lord, you are the God who was there in the beginning, through whom all things were made. We lift our hearts up to you in worship, praising you as the great I AM.

Amen.

4

I AM THE GATE

When Jesus healed a man blind from birth on the Sabbath, the Pharisees were outraged. They hauled the man into the temple and interrogated him. John had heard the report: news like this didn't stay a secret for long. The Pharisees wanted to know all about how Jesus had healed the man.

"He put the mud over my eyes," the man described, "and when I washed it away, I could see."

The miracle threw the Pharisees into confusion. John knew how seriously they took their authority

over God's people, and Jesus' miracles and teaching threatened them. If Jesus was from God, why would he heal on the Sabbath? And if he was not from God, how could he have healed this man?

"What's your opinion about this man who healed you?" the Pharisees demanded of the blind man.

But the man only knew one thing: he was blind, and now he could see. Wasn't that enough to show that Jesus was telling the truth about who he was?

Not for the Pharisees. John had heard that they threw the man born blind out of the temple. John knew how much they studied God's law, wanting to make sure that they—and the rest of Israel—remained pure and righteous by doing what God had commanded. But each new encounter they had with Jesus made John grow increasingly afraid of their hatred for Jesus. Jesus did not mince his words around them: he had already said that they weren't God's children and had even told them that the devil was their father!

John knew that the Pharisees wanted to arrest Jesus—they had even tried to stone him. And now, they took all their hatred for Jesus and piled it onto the man born blind, pushing him to the outside of the community.

The man was rejected and despised. John pitied him. Who would speak to him now, after he had been thrown out by the Pharisees?

John also felt fear creeping into his own heart. What would happen to him? What would happen to Jesus, if the Pharisees continued to work against him?

But John knew Jesus was not afraid. And Jesus did not forget the man he had healed but went to find him.

"Do you believe in the Son of Man?" Jesus asked the man.

"Who is he, sir?" the man responded. "I want to believe in him."

"You have seen him," Jesus said, "and he's speaking to you!"

Like John and so many others who had meet Jesus, the man responded to Jesus in worship. "Yes, Lord," he said, "I believe!"

Jesus told the man, "I entered this world to give sight to the blind and to show those who think they see that they are blind."

Nearby, a group of Pharisees overheard what Jesus and the man had said. They

took offense at Jesus' words. "Are you saying we're blind?" they asked, incredulous and angry.

Jesus responded with a parable.

"Anyone who sneaks over the wall of a sheepfold, rather than going through the gate, must surely be a thief. But the one who enters through the gate is the shepherd of the sheep, and the sheep recognize his voice. He calls his sheep by name, and they follow him because they know his voice."

John glanced around him as Jesus finished his story. He saw his own confusion reflected in the faces of those around him: what was Jesus talking about? Blindness, and now sheep? John was a fisherman, so he didn't know much about sheep. He had relatives who looked

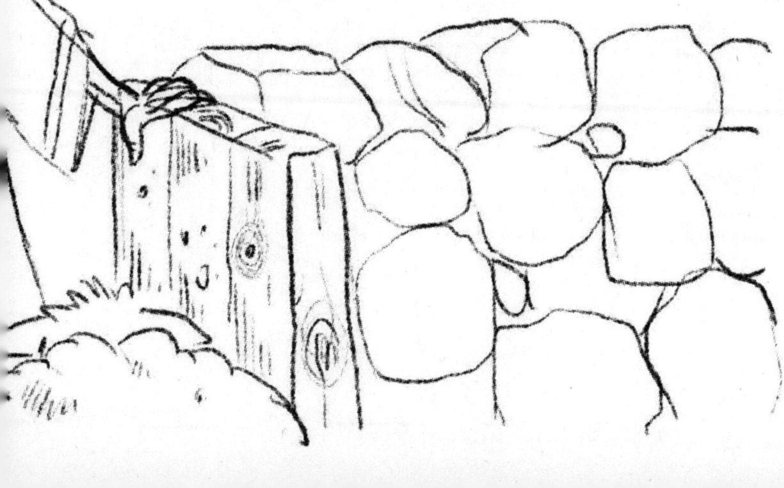

after sheep, though, and he remembered seeing the stone walls built to protect the sheep at night from wild animals, and the narrow opening to get in and out.

Like John, Jesus noticed the people's confusion, and so he continued to explain. "I tell you the truth, I AM the gate for the sheep. Those who come in through me will be saved."

John watched the man Jesus had healed, who still stood next to Jesus. What good words for him! He saw the way that the man looked at Jesus, with confidence and trust. Despite the anger of the Pharisees, despite the way they glared at him with narrowed eyes, the man was not afraid.

Jesus continued: "Those who come in through me will come and go freely and will find good pastures."

Even though the man Jesus had healed was rejected by the religious leaders, he was not rejected by Jesus. Instead, he was safe, protected from every danger, as precious to Jesus as a sheep is to his shepherd. John felt his own earlier fears subside as he knew that these words were for him, too.

GROWING DEEPER

JOHN 9:1 – 10:13

God's people knew about shepherds and sheepfolds. They also knew about gates and doors. They often sang about them in the Psalms, and the prophets had spoken of them, so those images were fixed in their hearts and their minds. They were images connected to the Messiah, the king who was to come. He would enter through the gates to the city of God, the city of righteousness, leading his people to enter as well. When Jesus came, he told the people, I'm not only the king who was to come, I'm also the way you get into the city of God. I'm the door, the gate. Come through me and be saved.

For those who come to Jesus, he gives not only safety and salvation, but freedom as well. Picture the sheepfold in the early morning. The sun is rising, and the dangers of the night are gone: the wolves have retreated to their dens, and thieves won't try anything in the daylight. Now, the shepherd lets the sheep out from the sheepfold. They stream out, eager for space and fresh grass to which the shepherd will lead them.

In and out. In Jesus, we have safety, salvation, and freedom.

PRAYER

Lord, you are the king who has made a way for your people. We praise you for the way you care for us, providing all that we need and more. Help us to come to you, trusting in your goodness.

Amen.

5

I AM THE GOOD SHEPHERD

John was not surprised to see the growing crowd. Jesus' conversation with the healed blind man had turned into a conversation with others around them, including a group of Pharisees. John found this happening more often now. As Jesus' reputation grew, crowds were drawn to Jesus, pulled towards him like thirsty animals to a pool of fresh rainwater.

John noticed a couple of young men persistently making their way to the front of the crowd, to see

and hear better what Jesus was saying. Some people frowned as they realized what the young men were doing, but no one called them out. There was always a good bit of gentle pushing to the front as onlookers found ways to move slowly, but deliberately, past the ones in front of them.

Some of this, John knew, was pure curiosity; people liked entertainment, and Jesus' discussions with the Pharisees were nothing like the dry conversations about the law that they were known for. Some of it, though, went deeper. John could see on their faces how eager they were to be near to Jesus. They had seen, like the man Jesus had healed, Jesus' words proven true by his love.

But some of it was antagonism, a deep opposition to who Jesus was and what he taught. John could sense it now. Jesus' earlier hinting that the Pharisees were blind had caused the Pharisees to react in defensiveness. John noticed the crossed arms, the clenched fists. He felt his own body tense in anticipation of a confrontation.

Jesus, however, did not address the Pharisees directly. His face was serious and his voice firm, but his words were for the crowd.

"All who came before me were thieves and robbers," he said. "The thief's purpose is to steal and kill and destroy. My purpose is to give them a rich and satisfying life."

Then Jesus said, "I AM the good shepherd."

John saw the way the Pharisees stiffened at Jesus' words. He may not have addressed them directly, but John knew that they would feel accused. They took Jesus'

words as a challenge to their leadership of God's people.

Instead of caring for God's people, they were acting like thieves and robbers, treating God's people like prey. John thought of the Pharisee's Sabbath rules and tithing regulations that ended up only burdening the people, all the while creating loopholes to make things easier on themselves. John sensed, as he knew others did, that they wanted leadership for the power it gave them, not in order to serve the people. And they had just cast the man whom Jesus had healed out of the temple—they wanted only to use him for their attack on Jesus. When he wouldn't go along with it, they treated him as if he was worth nothing.

"The good shepherd," Jesus said, "sacrifices his life for the sheep."

The crowd in front of John faded away as Jesus' images filled John's mind. As Jesus continued to speak, describing himself as a shepherd, John imagined a young shepherd and his flock grazing on a hillside.

"I AM the good shepherd," Jesus continued. "I know my own sheep, and they know me, just as my Father knows me and I know the Father. So I sacrifice my life for the sheep."

Images of wolves attacking, of the shepherd defending the sheep with his rod, of being wounded by the wolves even as he tried to fend them off, all flashed through John's mind. That last image,

of the wounded shepherd, lingered in his mind as the noise of the crowd brought his attention back to the present.

The Pharisees had already walked off. John saw their heads bent towards each other as they went, no doubt furious at what Jesus had implied about them. The remaining people argued among themselves. Some were incredulous. They wrote Jesus off as a lunatic—"He's demon possessed!" they cried.

But others remembered Jesus' miracles. "This doesn't sound like a man possessed by a demon!"

they protested. "Can a demon open the eyes of the blind?"

The question hung in the air as the people turned back to their homes and their tasks for the day. John knew that many of them would be content to leave the question of who Jesus was unanswered. He thought about his old life in Galilee, of what he had left behind to follow Jesus. What would he be doing now, if he had

let the rumors about Jesus simply be an entertaining story? Even as he thought of his days fishing on the Sea of Galilee with his father and his brother, he did not regret leaving. Jesus was worth following.

GROWING DEEPER

JOHN 10:14–21

When God spoke about his people, he often used the image of sheep. Sheep are very needy animals; they don't take care of themselves very well. They rely on a shepherd to keep them safe and to provide food for them. While God is described as the true shepherd of his people, other leaders in Israel's history acted as shepherds on his behalf—people like Moses and King David. The Bible calls them good shepherds because they led God's people with love. But some shepherds did not lead with love. Instead of taking care of his sheep, the leaders took advantage of the people. The sheep remained sick, weak, and lost under these shepherds. The prophet Ezekiel had harsh words for these people. Because of them, God told Ezekiel of a day coming when God, the true shepherd of his people, would seek out his sheep and care for them.

Jesus was proclaiming, loud and clear, to God's people: I'm the one you've been waiting for! He was the promised shepherd, the one who would faithfully care for his sheep. Neither John nor the people knew it then, but Jesus would show that he meant exactly what he said. It *was* necessary for Jesus to sacrifice himself, and he would do it. He laid down his life for his sheep—for God's people, for you and me—so that we might live. He is our good shepherd: knowing us, caring for us, even dying for us. In his hands, we are safe.

PRAYER

Lord, you are the good shepherd who has laid down his life for us, your sheep. You know us perfectly, and you gave everything to save us. We are amazed by the way you love us.

Amen.

6

I AM THE RESURRECTION AND THE LIFE

Mary and Martha's hearts were heavy. Four days ago, they buried their brother, Lazarus. Now, they were at their home, surrounded by people who had come to comfort them. So many people. And yet, the one friend they had asked to come was not there. His absence only added to

their grief over Lazarus' death. They had sent word that Lazarus was sick. How could he stay away? How could he have ignored their call for him to come? Didn't he love them? Didn't he love Lazarus?

Then, the news came—he was coming! Mary stayed inside, but Martha couldn't wait. She went out to meet him.

"Lord!" she said. She couldn't keep her grief inside. "If only you had been here, my brother would not have died."

If only. How piercing her words must have been! She knew Jesus' power; she had seen him perform miracles and heal the sick. She knew that nothing was too hard for him—not even now. "I know that God will give you whatever you ask," she said.

Jesus felt her grief, and he comforted her. "Your brother will rise again," he told her.

Martha knew this, too. The Scriptures spoke of the resurrection of the dead at the end of time. She knew it, and she believed it, but it gave her little comfort. Her brother was dead *now*. Her heart was broken *now*.

But Jesus had not been talking about the end of time. He said to her, "I AM the resurrection and the life."

He told her, "Anyone who believes in me will live, even after dying. Everyone who lives in me and believes in me will never ever die. Do you believe this, Martha?"

Martha looked boldly at Jesus, declaring, "Yes, Lord, I have always believed you are the Messiah, the Son of God, the one who has come into the world from God."

Jesus called for Mary. She, too, had words of "if only" for Jesus. Their grief poured out in tears, and their friends and family with them wept, too. But Jesus had more than words for them.

"Where have you put him?" he asked the sisters.

"Lord, come and see."

The mourners followed Jesus, uncertain as to what he would do. Jesus felt their grief deep inside of him, and he wept with them all. The sting of Jesus' delay softened as Mary and Martha saw Jesus' grief.

Then, he asked for the stone to be rolled away.

Martha's face registered her horror. After all, Lazarus had been dead for four days. "The smell will be terrible!" she exclaimed.

"Didn't I tell you that you would see God's glory if you believe?" Jesus responded.

When the stone was rolled away, Jesus prayed, thanking God for hearing him. He called out loudly, "Lazarus, come out!"

And then, there he came—still wrapped in grave clothes, his hands, feet, and face wrapped in linen, but walking towards them!

Martha gave a startled cry and stumbled towards her brother. Mary hesitated, unsure if what she was seeing was real.

"Unwrap him and let him go!" Jesus told them.

Lazarus was alive! With his sisters at his side, Lazarus walked towards the house. As they passed Jesus, Mary looked away from her brother to the one who had called him from the grave. This man, she thought, was like no one else.

GROWING DEEPER

JOHN 11:1–44

In the story of Scripture, death has been the enemy of God's people, of every human, ever since Adam and Eve ate the fruit in the garden. Yet, God will not put up with death forever. In the fight against death, God will win—once for all, completely. More than that, God *has* won. It is finished, done with. Jesus' declaration, "I AM the resurrection and the life," does not simply mean that Jesus gives life. He is life itself and the grave could not hold him. Jesus let death win at first, but when God raised him from the dead, Jesus broke the power of death.

Still, while Lazarus was raised back to life, eventually he would die again. Maybe someone you love has died. We know, like Martha, that the dead will be raised at the end. Because of Jesus' victory, death has been defeated. When Jesus raised Lazarus, he acted out not only what will happen at the end, but also what has happened and is happening. Because Jesus is life itself, the life that he is and gives is a new way of life, a life which death cannot touch. Jesus has brought this end-of-time life into the present. It is not only a future hope; instead, we live in that life right now.

At the tomb that day, Jesus addressed Lazarus. "Come out," he told him. And, someday, Jesus will speak to all the dead who have believed in him. "Come out!" he will call, and death will lose its grip on God's people forever.

PRAYER

Lord, you are the resurrection and the life. We give you our grief over those we love who have died. We praise you for your victory over death. Help us to wait with hope for the day that death will be no more.

Amen.

7

I AM THE WAY, THE TRUTH, AND THE LIFE

The disciples were bewildered. As they sat together, sharing a meal before the beginning of Passover, things were not going as expected. First, Jesus had gotten up from supper and washed his disciples' feet. Washed

their feet—their dirty, smelly feet! John thought of the dusty, dirty roads they had walked on that day, and the way the water in Jesus' basin had immediately changed from clear to muddy brown. It was the job of a servant, but here Jesus, their teacher, their Lord, had done it.

Then, shockingly, Jesus had announced that one of them would betray him. At those words, the disciples froze, afraid to look around. John's thoughts raced. One of them—really? And who could it possibly be? Who could do such a terrible thing?

John glanced at Peter. Peter inclined his head slightly, insistently, towards Jesus, who was sitting next to John. John hesitated. He understood what Peter wanted him to do.

"Lord, who is it?" John heard the eagerness in his voice and felt embarrassed. He couldn't meet Jesus' eye, even as his heart burned to know the answer.

But Jesus didn't hesitate in his answer. "It is the one to whom I give the bread I dip in the bowl," he replied. Then, he dipped the Passover bread into the bowl in front of him. He handed it to Judas, who was seated on Jesus' other side.

After Judas ate, Jesus spoke again, this time to Judas. "Hurry and do what you're going to do." Judas rose quickly, and John assumed that he was going to pay for their food. John looked around the room, this time furtively, Jesus' declaration of the coming betrayal still ringing in his ears. *None of these men,* John thought, *would be capable of that. Would they?*

As John turned this question over and over in his mind, he suddenly realized that Jesus was speaking again. John had missed the first part—something about glory.

But now, Jesus said, "You will search for me, but you can't come where I AM going."

This, John thought, was worse than everything that had come before. He was too stunned for words, but he caught the whispers that suddenly filled the quiet room. Exclamations of disbelief, questions of Jesus' intentions: no one understood what Jesus was talking about. After all, he was at the peak of his ministry. He had just raised a man from the dead. When Jesus had come to Jerusalem, the crowds had met him crying, "Hosana!" How could their hopes for a Messiah, a king to come and rescue them, be fulfilled if Jesus was going away? John had given up everything to follow Jesus. And now what?

Once again, Peter caught John's eye. This time, John shook his head: it was Peter's turn.

So, Peter blurted out, "Lord, where are you going?"

"You can't go with me now," Jesus replied, "but you will follow me later."

"But why can't I come now, Lord?" Peter asked. "I'm ready to die for you."

Jesus answered, "Die for me? I tell you the truth, Peter—before the rooster crows tomorrow morning, you will deny three times that you even know me."

John was dismayed—as were the others. Sensing their anxiety, Jesus continued. "Don't let your hearts be troubled. Trust in God, and trust also in me. There is more than enough room in my Father's home. If this were not so, would I have told you that I AM going to prepare a place for you? When everything is ready, I will come and get you, so that you will always be with me where I AM. And you know the way to where I AM going."

"No, we don't know, Lord," Thomas protested. "We have no idea where you are going, so how can we know the way?"

Thomas wanted a map. With so much upheaval, so many questions, this could not be left uncertain.

But Jesus answered, "I AM the way, the truth, and the life. No one can come to the Father except through me."

No map, no step-by-step directions. How could the disciples follow Jesus? How could they reach the Father, the house that Jesus said he was preparing for them?

Jesus' words echoed in John's mind. I AM *the way.* Hadn't he, hadn't all the others followed Jesus all along? How could Jesus leave them and still promise to be their way to God?

GROWING DEEPER

JOHN 14:1–14

Ever since Adam and Eve were banished from the Garden of Eden, people have been separated from God. Our sin makes it impossible for us to live with God, but God did not leave it at that. God reached out and provided the way. In Old Testament times, the sacrifices that God's people offered in the tabernacle and the temple gave them a picture of this way. The way back to God was costly, involving blood and sacrifice. The sacrifices—made day after day, month after month, year after year—pointed God's people to a better sacrifice, a better way to God: Jesus. He is the only way to the Father.

"I AM the way, the truth, and the life," Jesus told his disciples. They were given no map, no signs to point them in the right direction, no step-by-step instructions. None of that would have been enough. Jesus had to become the way, and he did so through his death and resurrection. In his death, he offered himself as the perfect sacrifice for his people. In his resurrection, he broke the power of sin and death. To get to the Father, we must follow Jesus. It's not enough to know something in our heads and agree to it. Instead, we need to be in relationship with the one who is the way, the truth, and the life. Only by our lives being bound to his can we get to the Father.

Eventually, the disciples would follow Jesus to the Father. They wouldn't need a map, and they wouldn't need directions. All they needed was Jesus.

PRAYER

Lord, lead us to the Father. Help us to cling to you—not to what we can do or what we know, but to you.

Amen.

I AM THE TRUE VINE

[illegible]

suspended at [illegible] each of his branch[illegible]

with their [illegible] plates [illegible]

the [illegible]

[illegible] of [illegible]

[illegible]

8
I AM THE TRUE VINE

For a few moments, John felt as if the room was suspended in time. The meal, each of his friends with their nearly empty plates, the muted noise from the street outside—everything halted abruptly as the weight of Jesus' words pressed on him. Jesus' words felt at once incomprehensible and absurd, leaving John—and the others—speechless. The silence of the twelve of them felt unnatural, especially when more than a few were clearly impatient with the desire to take action.

Yet, what was there to say? Jesus was going away. They were losing their teacher, their friend—and hadn't he promised to be their shepherd?

The flurry of questions racing through John's mind quieted as he realized that Jesus was speaking again. He tried to focus on Jesus' words, his encouragement: don't worry, don't be afraid. Jesus was telling them that even though he was going away, and even though they couldn't follow him right then, they wouldn't be left alone. He spoke of a helper, the Holy Spirit, who was coming in his place, to dwell in them.

"I AM in my Father, and you in me, and I in you," Jesus told them. "All who love me will do what I say. My Father will love them, and we will come and make our home with each of them."

Keep my word. For John, this was not new. This was part of his identity, after all, as part of God's people: keeping the words that God had given to them. But it also left him uneasy. How was he to do this? He knew

his people's history. He knew the history of Israel: it wasn't pretty. Again and again, the people whom God had called to obey him and live according to his word failed. They didn't obey God, and they weren't faithful to him. How could this time be any different?

Jesus gave them a picture of what he meant.

"I AM the true grapevine, and my Father is the gardener."

Vines, a vinedresser—the image was a familiar one to John. Asaph, one of King David's musicians, had sung about God bringing a vine out of Egypt and driving out nations in order to plant it and let it flourish. This vine, of course, was Israel, God's people.

John recalled the prophets who came after Asaph, who told the story of Israel, the vine. After God brought the vine out of Egypt, he did everything to cause it to flourish: he planted it in good soil near abundant water, and he built a wall around it to protect it. Then he looked for good fruit, for an abundant crop. God wanted the vine to grow so abundantly that it would spread into the

neighboring countries, to include them in their fruitfulness.

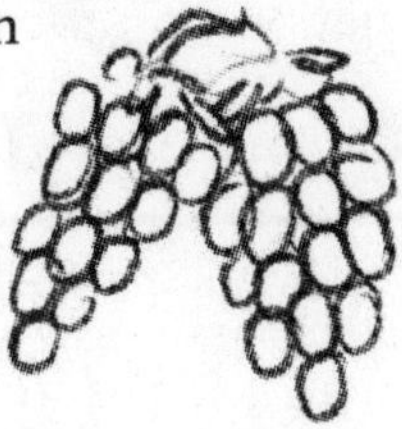

Yet, John knew, the vine that God had so carefully tended did not give good fruit. Instead, its produce was useless. Even though God had taken care of his people, had given them everything they needed to be fruitful, they turned away from God instead of keeping his word.

How could this time be different? Except—his head snapped up to look at Jesus—suddenly John realized that Jesus' picture was different from the one in the Psalms and the prophets. Before, it had been God's people who were the vine, and God was the vinedresser. Now, it was Jesus who was the vine—not the disciples.

"Remain in me," Jesus said, "and I will remain in you. For a branch cannot produce fruit if it is severed from the vine, and you cannot be fruitful unless you remain in me."

What would they have to do to reverse the pattern of unfruitfulness? What would they have to do to keep from being cast off and thrown into the fire? To these questions, Jesus answered, "I AM the vine."

As branches, the disciples would bear fruit simply by staying connected to the vine, to Jesus. Remain. Stay. Abide. The answer to their unfruitfulness wasn't to do more, to be more busy and more careful and more worried about whether or not they were doing the right thing and doing enough of it. Instead, Jesus told them, stay close to me. Get what you need to live from me.

Yet, John wondered, how could they do this when Jesus was going away? He thought of the helper that Jesus had spoken of. He wasn't entirely sure who Jesus was talking about, and how that helper would keep them close to Jesus. Still, as he continued to listen, he knew that Jesus would not abandon them. John may not know what that would look like or how it would turn out, but he knew the rabbi he had given up everything to follow. John loved Jesus. And as he looked around the table at the concerned and confused faces of the men he had spent his life with over the past few years, he knew that Jesus loved each of them—that Jesus loved *him*.

He recalled something Peter had said, almost at the beginning of their time with Jesus. Many people who had started to follow Jesus had decided to leave, and Jesus had asked them, the twelve, if they would leave, too. Peter's response had stuck with John: "Lord, to whom would we go? You have the words that give eternal life."

To whom would they go? Yes, John would not leave Jesus. And he felt certain, despite his talk of going away, that Jesus would not leave them, either.

GROWING DEEPER

JOHN 14:15 – 15:11

The image of the vine is threaded through Scripture. Despite its fertile land and the careful attention that God gives it, the vineyard yields bitter grapes. After Jesus' death and resurrection, the apostle Paul wrote to the Galatians, comparing their lives to a plant that bears fruit. He described the fruit that comes from abiding in Jesus as love, joy, peace, patience, kindness, goodness, faithfulness, gentleness, and self-control.

Paul calls these the fruit of the Spirit because they are the result of the Spirit's work. The Holy Spirit is the helper that Jesus promised to his disciples. The Spirit is the one who kept them close to Jesus. Through the Spirit, the disciples—and us, too—could abide in Christ in order to bear fruit.

We will end up just like Israel when we try to be fruitful apart from Jesus. Our fruit will be sour, our crop good for nothing. But when we remain in Jesus, when we cling to him and his words as our very life, we can be sure that we will bear fruit. It may be a slow growth. It may be a painful process, as God the vinedresser lovingly prunes away the things in our lives that won't bear fruit. But when we are in Jesus, like branches connected to the true vine, we have all we need to be fruitful.

PRAYER

Lord, you who are the vine, keep us abiding in you. Fill us with your Spirit so that we may bear good fruit.

Amen.

WILL YOU FOLLOW JESUS?

At the end of his gospel, John tells us the reason why he told the story of Jesus. He wrote so that his readers would believe that Jesus is the Messiah, the Son of God, and that, in believing, they would have life in his name. John saw in each of these "I AM" statements that Jesus made—the bread of life; the light of the world; the great I AM; the gate; the shepherd; the resurrection and the life; the way, truth, and life; the vine—that Jesus was the fulfillment of all that Israel had hoped and longed for.

He saw that Jesus answered the promises and completed the pictures that God had given his people as a way to prepare them for the Messiah. And, when he came, Jesus spoke and acted in a way that said to everyone who knew those promises and remembered the stories of their ancestors, "I'm the one you've been waiting for!"

Jesus called John, the twelve disciples, and everyone who listened to follow him as their shepherd, as the way to the Father. He offered himself as lasting bread. He offered the safety of entering through him, the gate, and following him, the shepherd. And he offered the life that he not only brings, but is in himself. Because he is the great I AM, he brings light, life, and fruit to all who believe in him. This is what Israel had been waiting for, and John wanted God's people to read and know that Jesus was the Messiah.

This is where you and I come into the story. We may not be the Israelites that were waiting for God's promises to be answered, but God's promises are for the whole world—you and me included. While we imagine what it might have been like for the Israelites to hear and respond to Jesus, we must also respond for ourselves.

You see, the story is not over. It doesn't end with the last chapter in John's Gospel, with the last story about Jesus that John told. And so the question is, will you enter into the story? Jesus has prepared the way, and we must follow him.

Following him will not always be easy. When we follow Jesus, we die with him and are raised with him. John found out, like Jesus, that the darkness does not want the light to shine. Exiled from his home, John knew that the cost of following Jesus was high. The darkness still tries to extinguish the light so that evil and death will win.

But even though the story's ending is ahead of us, we know the ending!

Much later, in a vision, Jesus showed John the end of the story. Jesus will come again, and when he comes, every sad thing will come untrue. The darkness will be banished, and sin and death and tears and pain will be no more. God will live with his people forever.

Until then, Jesus calls us to follow him. When we follow him, he becomes our bread, our light, our door, our shepherd, our resurrection life, our way, and our vine. In him, we have all we need and—yes, it's true—more, abundantly more, than we need.

Amen. Come quickly, Lord Jesus.

[illegible]

finished, and sin and death and tears and pain will be no more. God will live with his people forever.

Until then, Jesus [illegible]. When we follow him, he becomes [illegible] our light, our [illegible], our shepherd, [illegible] the true way, and our [illegible]. In him we have all we need. And yes, it's [illegible]

[illegible]

Father God, [illegible]

ABOUT THE AUTHOR

Laura Cerbus is a theologian, teacher, and writer. She lives in Western Pennsylvania with her husband and three children.